TRUMP
SONNETS

Volume 2

33 commentaries, 33 dreams

Ken Waldman

TRUMP SONNETS

Volume 2

33 commentaries, 33 dreams

Ken Waldman

Ridgeway Press
Roseville, Michigan

Book Design: Jerry Hagins

Ridgeway Press
P.O. Box 120
Roseville, Michigan 48066

Acknowledgments:

"Trump, McConnell, Ryan, Sessions, Pence, Conway, DeVos, etc." published in *What Rough Beast* under the title "Republican Leadership."

Thanks, too, to the many bookstores and readers that enthusiastically greeted *Trump Sonnets, Volume 1*. You know who you are. Without your support, this book wouldn't have come to be.

Contents

I

II

III

Donald Trump: The Dream Before the Dreams

I caught myself on my television
screen. Sharp! A tape of being interviewed
by the tall guy with glasses. There were feuds
he was asking about — that day's edition
of The New York Times. *I said their mission*
was to wound me — the failed Times *called me crude,*
vulgar, not a single word how I've wooed
the most beautiful girls on earth and won
at whatever I do. The screen went blank
next and I yelled at the stupid TV,
clicked the damn remote, walked over and shook
the machine. Then I grabbed a knob, and yanked.
The knob broke in two. A crime to not see
the rest of the show and how fine I looked.

I

Trump, By the Book

Challenges what a common thesaurus
can do: lamebrained, schizo, preposterous,
bugged out, imbecilic, dense, ludicrous,
one and only *trumpus dinosaurus*,
shuddersome snake sneaking on golf courses,
ghoulish, disgusting, raunchy, ominous,
unprincipled, unfilled, unscrupulous,
ungracious, unmannerly, a chorus
of canards, whoppers, deceits, harrowing
abnormality, gruesome ding-a-ling,
wacko, weirdo, flake, kook, crank, malignant,
scurrilous, grabby, baneful, repugnant,
redefines polluted, perverse, synthetic,
unprofessional, bellicose, toxic.

Donald Trump: Dream #1

They love me. They do. And it's tremendous.
Great things on both sides of Fifth Avenue.
The biggest parade you could ever view.
Gigantic. I'm on a float, like Jesus
if that's your belief. I'm almost speechless.
They love me so, so much. Who ever knew
it would be like this? Melania, too,
in a low-cut black gown. She made a fuss
earlier, but that's forgotten. Her smile,
like a queen's. She's got her own style,
which everybody loves, though not as much
as mine. This proves I have the finest touch.
I know people. And, yes, now they know me.
The land of the brave. The home of the free.

Trump, McConnell, Ryan, Sessions, Pence, Conway, DeVos, etc.

It's the hypocrisy and shamelessness
that astounds. How can so many rich men
and women incriminate themselves again
and again? With wealth, you'd think they'd practice
restraint, or would mix the deviousness
with subtle smarts. But abomination
after abomination. God, how can
they not see they can't pass judgment unless
they themselves act with dignity? They'll stand
in front of a camera, a straight face,
no irony, and claim the opposite
of what they've said or done. I don't understand:
have they all gone to theater school and aced
the same damn class: *Assholes and Their Crazy Shit.*

Donald Trump: Dream #2

An unusual hazard, a big wall
in front of the third green. I played my wedge,
lifted the ball to I guessed the near edge,
hoped it would roll twenty feet to the hole.
I hit it just right. My Titleist ball
flew way high, dropped, I hoped, on that wide ledge
by the fringe. Fine as corned beef and cabbage.
After my partner's shot, I rode so tall
in the cart, but then the strangest thing ever.
That wall. I couldn't see the green. Not a thing.
We couldn't get by it either. Never
heard of such a thing on a golf course. No kidding,
the wall kept going and going. There was no
way through. Got in the helicopter though.

Upon Hearing the Trump Administration May Separate Children from Parents

Such utter lack of imagination.
No sense of poetry or metaphor.
After all, war is never simply war,
but portal to chaos and extinction.
Diplomacy is the steady engine
that maintains order. To keep a border
secure, don't build a wall; just fix the door
so hard-working friends can be welcomed in.
Yesterday I read of plans to separate
children from parents, those poor families
caught as illegals. That's the newest low,
one more tactic to sow anger, hate,
discord. It's a bully's idiocy.
More troops? More drones? I hear the drumbeats grow.

Donald Trump: Dream #3

I stood on the mound, Yankee Stadium.
My right arm was so loose it felt like gold.
I had a four-hit shutout going. My old
man stood facing me at the plate. Get 'em,
get 'em, I heard from the dugout. Yum Yum,
strike him out. More words. No runner to hold,
I went to my full wind-up, threw it cold,
a rude fastball that absolutely hummed
with filthy stuff. My daddy had to duck,
and he did, just in time. How he glared. Luck,
or I'd have hit him between the eyes. He looked
shaken like I'd never seen. He was spooked,
and why shouldn't he have been. I had his
number. I glared back. I knew I'd win this.

Trump, 45

How the office of the presidency
has been diminished. Washington, Lincoln,
Jefferson, Madison have this cretin
in their midst. If someone with such teensy-
weensy intellect and morals can be
commander-in-chief, why not Bart Simpson,
or Trump's Rasputin, Stephen K. Bannon?
Our new leader has a taste for fancy
domiciles in most expensive zip codes.
The crown prince of cruelty. The toad of toads.
Roosevelt, Truman, and this clown subtle
as a bulldozer. He thinks *rebuttal*
is posterior plastic surgery.
He's Alfred E. Neuman: *What, me worry?*

Donald Trump: Dream #4

I was in one of my airplanes, heading
to Scotland. And then I was somehow in
my New York City home. I'm uncertain
how it happened, but there was my bedding
with wife and daughter. It was a wedding.
Other women were there. Beautiful grins.
There was happiness. Such beautiful thin
women. One of them was sitting, reading
a story about me. Then I was flying,
but not to Scotland. Instead, Florida.
I was on the phone. Someone was buying
one of my hotels in California.
It was so easy closing the best deal
of my life. So vivid that it was real.

Trump, in Front of His Television

I imagine him watching furious,
thumbs tweeting rants on his trusty android.
The TV: the mirror he can't avoid.
Textbook narcissism, this curious
obsession with self, a truly vicious
air aimed at those who don't share his annoyed
conceits. In simpler times how he enjoyed
comedies. The networks weren't malicious
back then. He could view an hour, chuckling
at some chubby girl, an ugly duckling
delivering solid jokes. A pretty
girl, though, was much better. Pussy, kitty —
that's what he desires on screen. Not the news.
Fake TV! Bad people! Sad! No excuse!

Donald Trump: Dream #5

My late friend, Hugh Hefner, called me over,
saying he had someone very special
just for me. She was blonde. Voice like a bell.
Yellow bathing suit that barely covered
her pussy. She'd be mine. I could love her
any way I wanted. There is no hell
or that's where I'd be going. Oh how we fell
into bed — though I gave her a push, her
eyes telling me she wanted me right then
so I just had to oblige, and opened
that door. In that I'm a gentleman.
I know what it takes to please a woman.
I showed who's boss. I took all I wanted.
I took her like a herd of elephants.

Trump, and Education

This sad presidency, an indictment
of an education system and culture
that's ill. Ample stories foretold failure.
It was no secret how he skipped debts, bent
laws, went blithely on. His grim discontent:
pathologic. But what we can be sure:
he'll be as he's been—fraudster chieftain, pure
scoundrel reveling in each dark moment.
What needs teaching is critical thinking.
Instead, too much lame nodding and winking
to maintain a status quo that includes
substandard schools, their political feuds.
The hope: those millions of teens who won't buy
an unwell elder's lies and alibis.

Donald Trump: Dream #6

I'm in a joint serving Mexican food,
and, excuse me, it was full of people
I didn't know. It was really awful.
The food wasn't to my liking. Not good.
And no one knew me. If I could, I would
have left. But, no, it wasn't so simple.
No, not simple. Like an invisible
wall. I stood up and got shocked. But I stood
anyway, The owner came. Or the cook.
He was holding papers and a thick book
that were supposed to mean something special.
Looked to me like it was Mexican hell.
A man in uniform took me to jail.
There was not one lawyer. There was no bail.

Trump, Priority

His priority: buyers at Nordstrom—
how dare they drop his girl's clothes. Seattle
and its people can all go straight to hell
as far as he's concerned. Where he's from
they don't play politics with his girl. Dumb
to even try. His aim: to make people
sell Nordstrom stock. He'll whisper some things, tell
a secret he shouldn't. After all, come
look at their manipulations. His girl
is always a strong seller. Excellent
taste in fashion. Please, no one can quarrel
with that. Their tactics are so transparent.
What's wrong with Nordstrom is what's wrong elsewhere.
Worse than climate change and Obamacare.

Donald Trump: Dream #7

Everyone cheering, the biggest rally
I've ever had. Then I started to talk
and the sound system went down, a big squawk.
No one could hear. It was going badly.
People started fighting. There was no alley
being cleared for me. I started to walk,
flanked by agents. They guarded me like hawks.
I wanted to stay, but had to go, rally
or no rally. It had turned dangerous.
A helicopter appeared. Tremendous
idea. We rose up over the stadium.
They were little people, but lots of them.
I was sorry they couldn't hear me there.
I'd get the rest of my applause elsewhere.

Trump Family and Cruz Family Dine

The White House hosted Senator Ted Cruz
and family for a meal, according
to reports. Conservative Ted, sneering
rival, whose dad, Donald Trump once mused,
was a Lee Harvey Oswald pal. And whose
wife, Trump riffed, was an awfully plain thing
beside his Melania. This breaking
of bread by nasty shills the same old news.
We imagine the smallest talk between
the two women, who leave unsaid the mean,
mad insults of their calculating men.
Trump and Cruz, what a team. We imagine
sugary drinks thick as that border wall.
And Cruz's young daughter, taking in all.

Donald Trump: Dream #8

We were served plates of the most tender veal.
The plates kept coming and we kept eating.
We had the best table, the first seating
of the evening. A beautiful meal.
I sat with Ivanka and Eric, real
close together. We heard ourselves breathing.
Somehow it had turned into a meeting
and the kids wanted to know how to steal
Donald Jr.'s shares. It was hard to know
whether to be angry or proud. Follow
your daddy, I told them. The veal was good,
and chocolate cake too. I like my food
well-done, everything chewy but tender.
The cook knew some tricks. Our waitress, slender.

Trump, and His Cronies

God damn them, they don't ever stop, do they?
Such empathy, now dropping Meals on Wheels.
How can an office push for defense deals
worth trillions and at the same time okay
cutting hot food for seniors? That's one way
to measure the character of these eels,
though that's an insult to eels. They don't feel
a thing as they go about their days, say
to themselves what next. The Humanities,
the NEA, public radio too
could get zeroed out. Possibilities
are endless. Wait and see. Soon they'll argue
against libraries, the postal service,
the Peace Corps. All good deeds make them nervous.

Donald Trump: Dream #9

I was in a room of papers and books.
Nice enough shelves and chairs, but still nowhere
I'd want to be. There were no doors, but stairs,
which I walked up. There were windows. I looked
out, but it was dark. I had what it took
to get out, but I didn't know how. My hair
wasn't right, so I combed it. I took the stairs
down. Another room. More papers and books.
I reached for my phone, but it was gone. Gone!
I shouted for Melania. I'm done
here, I shouted. Let me out of here now!
I heard the echo. Who could have allowed
this to happen? I would have to fire them.
I needed to telephone the Kremlin.

Trump, and His Wall

Quintessential Trump: that Mexico wall,
a perfectly divisive exercise.
Metaphor, too, for weird logistics and lies.
It's supposed to be thirty feet tall—
more than two stories high—and prevent all
climbers, tunnelers, and random bad guys
from crossing. The best wall our money buys.
Bigger than Berlin or China, it *shall*
show our might. Better than fixing bridges,
and roads. Better than supporting music,
literature, or art. Better than pouring
money into schools. Like digging ditches,
but high and thick instead of deep. Tons of brick
or concrete. Sure beats treating global warming.

Donald Trump: Dream #10

I was back to being a little boy.
Like Barron now, but completely different.
I was on my way to a black-tie event,
the kind of party I always enjoy,
but I was short, and carrying a toy.
Melania looked like my mother. Gents
were eyeing her close. One man even went
so far as to tremendously annoy
me by putting a hand on her rear end.
I saw him do it so I kicked him hard
in the shin, and then I did it again
and again until someone called a guard
and tossed me out. Melania didn't
bat an eye. My revenge I can't say in print.

If Not Trump

The United States Congress has all sorts
of power to contain this president
if it wished. So it's no solo accident,
his policies and picks. The show of force
is not his alone. At some point the courts
can limit or delay his worst judgments,
but this is the partisan government
that swapped Gorsuch for Garland like a sports
trade. The men and women who would allow
such a thing would compromise how
much more. If there weren't a Donald Trump,
there would be another we'd have to bump
heads with. At least this president is so
transparent: his Ivanka and Jared show.

Donald Trump: Dream #11

I was in my tower watching TV.
The best of the old Miss America
contests. That was great. Miss Indiana
looked like my daughter, Ivanka. Let me
say how pretty they all looked. So pretty.
Miss Maryland. Miss Louisiana.
I was thirty again. Miss Virginia
made me really look. So did Tennessee.
I turned the channel. The Miss Universe
contest was even better. All the girls
from every nation. It's almost a curse
being young and rich as I am. Girls
everywhere. Miss Ireland. Miss Netherlands.
Russia, Egypt, The Philippines, Scotland.

Trump, as Daddy

What kind of father was the president?
Absent, though his kids wouldn't admit that.
Rarely home, how he'd spoil them, his wee brats,
then be gone weeks, squeezing fifty per cent
profit on a dollar from Euro gents,
Midwest scions, rich Asians. He'd do what
he'd always do, big-shot tycoon, the fat cat
dealer with a brand on all continents.
Epic operator, he bought fortune,
sold misery. Then home to the children,
whom he'd spank with zeal if they displeased him,
or inadvertently disobeyed him.
Now he fancies himself George Washington
with his own Uncle Sam, Mr. Steve Bannon.

Donald Trump: Dream #12

Every time I hit the driver, a slice,
and it was getting worse. 3rd hole, 4th hole,
5th hole, 6th hole where the ball even rolled
out of bounds. I swung hard. Another slice
even further to the right. Jesus Christ,
I took out a three iron. A total
shank. I snapped that club — the sport takes its toll.
When I walked off the course, it wasn't nice —
broken club, lost balls, a sad afternoon
which I never wanted to live through again.
That damn slice! I felt like such a buffoon.
What I needed was the perfect woman,
so texted my fair and beautiful wife.
Soon she was in my arms. My clubhouse life.

Trump, the Model

How to explain this to the smarter kids:
If their United States president
is proud bully and liar, it follows that government
has chosen to reward such. What he did—
that's what they ought to do. Right? Grab, cheat, hit,
kick, be cruel, threaten suits, throttle dissent
with fists, call violent acts sad accidents.
Smart kids mimic adults. They're not stupid.
To reach the top, smart kids can see it means
stealing a classmate's burrito. Or means
punching rivals in the stomach, making
fun of an accent, ganging up, breaking
glasses. In Montana it means proudly
body-slamming writers, then griping loudly.

Donald Trump: Dream #13

A bluegrass band was playing, a racket
like I never heard. Spare me the banjo —
I prefer bagpipes, or a piccolo,
or a bugle. That fiddler, a ticket
to madness. Couldn't someone just crack it,
that piece of wood, in fifty pieces. Oh
god, all I had was a ripe tomato,
which was in a pocket of my jacket.
So I aimed at the band with all my might.
My right arm wasn't what it used to be.
The tomato splattered before the stage.
In another pocket somehow a white
rock. I took it out. It felt good to me.
Good weight, heft. I threw again. That's courage!

Are You a Trump Man?

October 2016, window seat,
a flight from Spokane to Las Vegas,
the woman beside me asked if I was
local, then if I was *a Trump man*. Sweet,
the irony. I mulled whether to repeat
the week's news and grab pussy, breast, and ass,
or otherwise bully and harass
my neighbor. Ah, a Trump man! Folding a sheet
of newspaper, I chose to ignore
the question. She asked once more, then hissed
to the man on the aisle, *So he's for
Hillary, the murderer.* I resisted
responding, glanced back at the op-ed piece,
an argument to privatize police.

Donald Trump: Dream #14

I was in my airplane — how I love flying
to any of my homes. I was so content.
Everyone below: their car accidents,
their wars. Such problems. And people dying —
not my problem. My pilot was crying,
and I saw with utter astonishment
it was my elder brother. Had he been sent
from hell? Dead for years, now he was eyeing
me between the tears. I could parachute,
I thought, or wrestle him and take control
of the aircraft. Get me a gun — I'd shoot
him. He just kept crying. I have a soul,
I thought, as the plane lost altitude then.
It wasn't a question of if, but when.

Trump, in Perspective

For those who once asked how Saddam Hussein
could rule Iraq with such flimsy support,
just take a look at the American courts,
the congress, the media, the insane
culture that elected a cad whose plain
knack is to make chaos and thievery sport.
How he's desecrated the stage. Yes, snort
at the antics. But as he entertains
the latest outrageous declarations
that threaten the US, and all nations
of this angry world, when do we dump him
and put a match to the ugly junk bin
surrounding him: enablers in congress,
slick yes-men, slack judges, the far-right press.

Donald Trump: Dream #15

In the limo, suddenly the headlights
went out. We sped forward in a darkness
darker than I'd ever known. I confess
I wanted to fire the damn chauffeur right
then and there. No headlights. It was midnight
or just after. I realize this makes no sense,
but I was there and could only guess, yes,
the world had ended. Had I taken flight?
Had we dropped a bomb, one of the big nukes
I'd sometimes discussed with the generals?
No headlights. Very dark. I could have puked
and then I did. What a mess. I was full
of something nameless. Darkness. A blackness.
And then the limo stopped. I was undressed.

Trump Spokesperson

The hapless press secretary. Poor man
having to stand in front of reporters
and daily parrot profane headquarter
policy. He's the glorified doorman,
the sorry rep, propaganda's foreman.
How his patience grows shorter and shorter—
every day a peeved horde of reporters
shout questions to trip him up. A sore man,
an unhappy man, the compromised agent
who has to tell untruths and invent
the most super-absurd explanations
for such torturous conduct. His chieftain's
public face, he's a useless suit, sad sack
mouthpiece for a mad fascist maniac.

Donald Trump: Dream #16

What was I supposed to do? I'm naked
in a creek, and have to take a big dump.
So I squat and move my bowels. A long lump —
a big beautiful lump — mostly gold, red
streaks. Not a great smell, but what have I said,
I'm not just anyone. I'm Donald Trump.
I'm happy to do my job, whether jump
on a plane, or else squat in this creekbed.
My father told me the world is oyster.
Everything I say or do is a pearl.
A beautiful pearl, my dad's big voice. Sir,
I say, pointing proudly, as if at a girl.
That's quite a shit, my boy, he says loudly;
I tell him I'll do it again, daddy.

II

Donald Trump: Dream #17

Deep underwater and I was drowning.
This was serious. I just couldn't breathe.
I looked. I was in a glass bowl. My teeth
were white. Perfect teeth! I wasn't clowning.
No, not funny at all. I was downing
water. I was going to die. My death,
I could feel it. Oh god, I couldn't breathe.
And the onlookers. It was astounding
how they could watch and not do anything
to help. My mother. My father. Nothing.
They did nothing. Melania was watching
too. And Ivanka. Eric was catching
it on video. So was Donald Junior.
I couldn't swim. I was sunk forever.

To Mitch McConnell, Trump Instrument

You deserve your own very special poem,
you, the foul confederate. I wonder
what made you such a vile avuncular
thug of a lawmaker. How you'd entomb
poor folks in Louisville, Lexington, some
eastern Kentucky mountain hamlet under
cover of night. You love the carpenter,
Jesus Christ, but would you ever welcome
him into your home? You're famous, you know.
A Seattle friend said she'd sacrifice
her life just to see you forever gone.
Sir, you privately say it's all for show,
this political theater. Move your piece,
senator, you disgusting, spiteful pawn.

Donald Trump: Dream #18

Green sky. Green faces. Everywhere such green.
Green. It's my second favorite color.
Favorite of my mother and father,
and their dearest friends. You know who I mean:
CEOs, millionaires, princesses, queens.
Everything green, including my mother —
her hair, lipstick, teeth. Even the butler
was green, the most brilliant I'd ever seen.
Then I saw the green funnel in the sky.
I watched as that wind took everything in
and came toward me. Green wind. I wondered why
now. Was it my time? The craziest wind.
Then it turned left, away from the high ground
where I stood. The windstorm turned everything brown.

Trump's Attorney General

Jefferson Beauregard Sessions, courtly
southern gent on the surface, a weasel
beneath. Grab a canvas and an easel,
paintbrush and paints. Color the deep cruelty,
the dark crookedness, the civility
that's short for meanness and greed. The measles
is too good for him. Instead, paint upheaval —
surround him with black people; make them sporty,
happy, rich, minding their own sweet business.
The white man's face: between thin smile and snarl.
The painting's background suggests a racist
engaged in deep interior quarrels.
Perhaps a clean white robe and hood hanging
in a closet; a black robe, too, for changing.

Donald Trump: Dream #19

There were peach trees. I'm a big fan of fruit.
Certain kinds. How I love a juicy plum.
And cantaloupes are so round and wholesome.
Girls I like — they think a banana is cute
(they've told me I own a big, meaty brute).
And the ripened cherry. Where I come from
that's the ultimate snack. We all want some
and do what it takes. I wore my new suit,
but there was not a single cherry tree.
Just peach trees. Row after row of peach trees.
Normally I love how peaches and cream
taste. So rich. But this was the strangest dream.
The peaches were talking. I had no doubt —
screwball peaches. No cream. I wanted out.

Trump, Innuendo

What's with all the Russian men getting killed?
Manhattan, DC, Moscow, the Ukraine—
bashed heads, shootings, a fall, It shows real brains
and an utter ruthlessness to fulfill
these contracts. The deaths will continue until
every last threat is silenced. So again
we'll see some lawyer, diplomat, or main
witness in an investigation filled
with secrets meet a both predictable
and sudden end. How are we unable
to protect these guys, get them to trial
so they can say what they know? It's the wild
west of global politics. For rich men
in power, what's an assassination?

Donald Trump: Dream #20

The bodies that had disrespected me
were lined up in front. I took a pistol
and shot them. I heard shouts, then a whistle.
Finally I'd done it. My god, finally,
and it felt like I could fly. I was free
at last. I wanted to break out crystal
and celebrate. Where was my wife? Missiles,
I wanted to shoot missiles, too. I could be
king. One hundred per cent obedience.
Where was my queen? Melania, I yelled.
Who showed up but my assistant, Mike Pence.
Where was Melania? I yelled and yelled.
I couldn't believe it. I'll divorce her,
ungrateful woman. Then we'll deport her.

Trump, To Be Made King

Making the rounds, a rumor that right-wing
zealots are marshaling forces to call
a states' convention to shred the whole
U.S. constitution. With everything
else happening—daily chaos claiming
full attention—nothing seems impossible,
even this, so outright unthinkable.
The plan: though legally called, hijacking
such a gathering would be quite simple.
Under the guise of balancing the budget,
erasing debt, the ones in charge can sidestep
congress and the courts, rewrite the total
document. Sounds like fiction, doesn't it?
Or a Sundance downer with Johnny Depp.

Donald Trump: Dream #21

There was darkness. Darkness. There was no light,
no light switch. But I carried a matchbook,
so took a match and struck. Okay, I took
another match when the first flame died. Right
then I got smart. What are we without sight?
I lit a match. It was that easy. Look,
I could see. I lit a big shelf of books,
then the curtains. It was the edge of night.
It was getting hot though. I found the door,
went out. Why I didn't do that before,
I don't know. It was a beautiful day.
Blue sky. No clouds. A perfect day to play
golf, but for all the smoke. Terrible how
fires do massive damage when winds blow.

Trump, Redefined

It's only a matter of time before
certain truths get defined as *parallel*:
a judicial bribe—just a buy-and-sell;
obstruction of justice—that's minding the store;
money laundering—clean suits for some poor
mistreated boys. We can all go to hell
though it will still be called our most special
democracy. New war? Old war? A war
is no longer a war but the right to be
who we are. We aren't mad. We're no bully.
The United States of America
savors its *parallel* ways. Obama
has been put in place. All hail President
Donald Trump. A most superior gent.

Donald Trump: Dream #22

Outside my front door, a small dead brown bird.
I thought to myself, stupid little thing —
remove it quickly. I wasn't having
anything like that near me. I gave word
to my people, but no one came. Absurd,
it was absurd. Dead, dumb little brown thing
lying in front of my door. Broken wing?
I didn't know. I just knew what occurred
shouldn't have. No back door, no garage, no way
out except to sidestep the body. Say
what you will, but it was so disgusting.
So I gripped my five iron, took a swing,
knocked the feathered mess to the street. Best shot
I'd hit in weeks. A birdie. I've had lots.

Trump, Truth

From this White House we've learned the enemy
is truth. If something is true, it's truly fake,
at least as I've now come to fully make
sense of their views. *It's a conspiracy,*
the White House says, *from judiciary*
to media to the Muslims who break
laws being here, who aim to overtake
this exceptional land. This great country
can only be great by fighting harder,
fighting tougher, by being much smarter
than the others. We're much more powerful.
We're bigger — more bombs if not more people.
The strength is real truth! That's not fake at all!
Death to newspapers! Journalists to jail!

Donald Trump: Dream #23

The checks. They were for such little money.
Now they want to talk to me about them.
Never before has this been a problem.
Is this a joke? Some ha-ha-ha-ha funny
thing? I don't like to joke about money.
It's crass is what it is. Must be some Dem
maneuver. 10 dollar checks! A problem,
they tell me. Do they think I'm some dummy
they can investigate about nothing?
A stack of 10 dollar checks. I'm minding
my business. I'm used to minding millions
of dollars. What am I saying? Billions.
Billions! I woke sweating like some damn bum.
Tell me where these cheap images come from.

Trump, the Airwaves

National Propaganda Radio
I heard a good friend describe NPR
some years back. I'll still listen in the car,
noting how several daily talk shows
feature more conservative guests who'll go
on about North Korea, Iraq, Qatar.
Always a case for added troops, more war.
There's only so much we can fully know.
But please don't tell me the conservative
right is the middle. Don't ask me to give
this president one more chance. Because still
we'll be told the network is liberal.
The brainwashing is so insidious.
Choose Amy Goodman instead. She'll resist.

Donald Trump: Dream #24

The power was out. We had one more hour
to nightfall. What we did to each other
I'd never done or had done. Remember,
I'm married, I told her. Then you'll shower
afterward, she said. We went back to our
most delicious business. Oh brother,
could she turn it on. We made each other
into the world's greatest super-power,
and I was fine with that. I would never
cheat on Melania. But forever
was so long. No name. No face. But those lips
and that Miss America voice. Zip
it back up, she said. I'm having such fun,
I said, and I won't leave before I'm done.

Trump as Child Star

Such wild rumors: staffers have to babysit
the president, treat him as spoiled brat,
use psychology, say exactly what
he wants to hear. He's not just a nitwit,
it seems, but he can't be left a minute
alone, or he'll get into mischief that
gets repeated hourly. The man's flat
mind tends to TV and Twitter. Can it
even comprehend the fire and gore
of first-strike, all-out nuclear war?
Who has his back? The man's chief advisors
are an historic cast of bad actors.
And the president: deranged little boy
playing both flaky pest, aimless decoy.

Donald Trump: Dream #25

They were clapping and laughing. All those laughs.
I didn't understand. I waved my hand,
gave them my best smile. These were my big fans,
a full stadium. Then I saw my staff—
they were laughing too. Great big and hard laughs.
But what's funny? I didn't understand.
This had nothing to do with the day's plan.
Then the signal for me to cut in half
the fair maiden in the box beside me.
I took the saw and went at it quickly.
I cut her in two. Ha, it was Mother Earth.
That was funny. Or rather Grandma Earth,
which made it funnier. The old broad's corpse
stunk, and her pale arms were covered with warts.

Trump, and His Generals

How he loves talking about his generals.
Talking? Oh, it's one more reason to brag
on his all-day, all-night POTUS hash-tag.
His generals? That's his improbable
euphemism for kingly genitals.
He might as well proclaim them his stags,
his response to mundane duties that nag
and nag. The yes-sir straight-backed generals
do his full bidding. Is that what they learned
at West Point, the generals? Have they earned
stripes by putting career over country?
I'd have thought they'd have studied history.
How can they let their commander play them?
At what point coup instead of orgasm?

Donald Trump: Dream #26

I'm the only one in the lecture hall,
hundreds of empty seats surrounding me.
No one else is in the big room. Just me,
and my father's up front, talking. He's tall,
taller than I remember. I recall
a scene from long ago, my family
fighting mad. Mother, father, brother, me,
and my sister. We needed a big wall
so we wouldn't kill each other. Father
stood in front of us in that old picture,
scolding that we were no good, none of us.
Crying hard in the corner, my brother
didn't understand this was our nature.
I did, so father gave me an A-plus.

Trump, and Pundits

I love how the pundits don't know what's next.
It's no accident, Mr. President,
they don't know if you just came or went.
You're the master of discord. Oh, you're vexed
at the press yet again, miffed that some text
got leaked. But what do you expect? Permanent
chaos defines the perpetually bent
out of shape you, clutching phone, tweeting the effects
of grand arcana. *Covfefe*? It's time
for a poetry both old and new. How
else to process such an inane clutter.
William Butler Yeats—he wrote so sublime
about a center that's been lost. Allow
this indulgence: Trump, you're sicko fucker.

Donald Trump: Dream #27

So many people sleeping in the streets.
Yellow school buses were lined up in rows,
waiting. Where were all the children? Who knows?
Some were with parents, lying in the streets.
The others must have been lost. All the seats
in the buses were empty. God, all those
sad failures in the streets, bundled in clothes,
bags around them. Someone was grilling meats
by a truck, and there was a big, long line
of men, women. No kids. Some dogs. A blind
man was begging. I'd seen this on my phone
and my TV. Had I found a war zone?
I turned and began walking. Dogs, debtors.
Each step further away, I felt better.

Trump, in Comparison

My friend in Germany wrote they've seen this
before: crackpot without majority
support, taking firm rein of a country
to turn up the heat, make a big furnace,
put flame to what most hold dear. People miss
what they love for awhile. But it's easy
to adjust, and forget. Security
and safety first! The homeland replaces
love and trust. People can be so fearful—
en masse they'll do anything. The answer
is to read, write, talk to a neighbor.
We'll beat this. The news may be terrible,
but truth is stronger than this immense cancer.
Trump is Dick Nixon. Not Adolph Hitler.

Donald Trump: Dream #28

There was a cage. It might have been a zoo.
Surrounding me were turkeys, pigs, donkeys,
ducks, snakes, goats, several kinds of monkeys.
I was hungry. I didn't know what to do
so I rattled the cage real hard. A few
of the animals made noises at me.
I kept rattling the cage. It was crazy.
This was no zoo. I'd been thrown in jail. Who
the hell put me here? I rattled the cage
one more time. A fat guy about my age
came over. He wore a white uniform,
and carried a big stack of yellow forms.
Your papers, he said, and set them outside
the cage, left a pen, said I could decide.

Trump, On Duty

He presides over mudslide, bloodshed, flood,
tornado, blizzard, every condition
of American life. His decisions
can change a life, change the world, make a good
place better, a bad place worse. It's the food
we eat, the air we breathe. Television,
radio, the internet. Collision
of millions of people, millions of moods,
daily opportunities and crises,
threats from climate change, terror, new disease.
He presides as deer caught in headlights,
a bright few seconds of otherworldly sight
before the sudden crash, impact, and thud
of tragedy. Oceans of gunk and crud.

Donald Trump: Dream #29

I saw an owl, picked up a gray feather
from the ground. There were more birds in a tree.
Big, small. Gray, white, black. I could only see
some of them. It was time without weather,
just me, the birds, and the gray owl feather.
One white bird took off and swooped down toward me.
Another did the same. A small army
of birds, one after another. Either
they all veered off or somehow disappeared
in flight until a big old gray owl neared
and attacked. The bird came at me again
and again. Such an abomination.
That horrible owl had a knack for drama.
Gray face like the wiretapper, Obama.

Trump Bumper Sticker

A disabled veteran's license plate —
a Trump/Pence sticker. I wonder
how this vet views these long months of thunder
and lightning, a president who spews hate,
creates policies that eviscerate
the government. Equal parts blunder
and darkness. A vulgarian's plunder.
So this is to make America great
again. And the vet in the old pick-up
in front of me. I wonder: Did he give up
a limb? Suffer PTSD? His wounds,
what form do·they take? Do random loud sounds
make him cry? Such a ludicrous season.
Diminished nation. Probable treason.

Donald Trump: Dream #30

In the elevator I pushed 19,
but we were going down, not up, faster
than I'd ever known. Like a disaster
movie. Or the terrible final scene
in a story from a tabloid magazine.
I kept going down faster and faster
inside the dark box. Faster and faster
down the shaft. Seconds, then minutes between
whatever was before and whatever
was after. I kept going down. Never
had I imagined anything like this.
It was dark. I was nowhere. How I missed
my homes, my golf courses, all the people
who needed me. Then it all turned purple.

Trump's American Dream

When will we become refugees who flee
for Mexico, Canada, or Finland?
Post-Brexit, it certainly won't be England,
Scotland, Northern Ireland. Germany
perhaps. Maybe Spain, Italy. We'll see
where it goes. The Southern wall we pretend
will keep people out, will trap us in, friends.
Where to go when others treat us as we
treat them? Perhaps we'll turn into Turkey
with coup — maybe real or just as likely
designed by state — thwarted in order
to consolidate power. Our borders
could close both ways. Why not? It's sure to get
worse once we start on tax reform and debt.

Donald Trump: Dream # 31

I was wearing a great big crown. All gold
and everybody bowed down. Korea,
Germany, Italy. Mama-Mia!
Mine, all mine. I didn't have to be told.
Did I tell you I wore a crown? All gold.
They bowed down in Pakistan, India,
Mexico, Canada, California.
Mine, all mine. I was twenty-five years old
again. That was when I was most potent
and I was surrounded by all my queens,
the most beautiful and intelligent
women ever. The stuff of magazine
cover stories. I was the greatest king.
Did I mention the gold crown I was wearing?

Trump, Russia Probe

No collusion, you say. Why believe you
when we can make a quick list and recall
prior false claims: crowd size, wiretaps, et al.
So foul, your misplaced gall. Why believe you
who traffics in alternative facts? Who
habitually confuses *big* and *small*?
Whose demented antics dismiss most all
science? You've squandered your capital, you
who's acted extra-guilty from the start.
An innocent man welcomes tough review,
wouldn't fire capable staff, wouldn't act
like he had something grim to hide. Let's chart
chronology, statements, then parse what's true:
hackings, iffy meetings, to-be-learned facts.

Donald Trump: Dream #32

A big stage, me with Batman, Superman,
Popeye, and a trim Miss America.
That was Candy from South Carolina.
Batman called me a real American,
said I was more potent than Superman.
Candy called me Mr. America,
said I should move to South Carolina.
I owned every last thing, not just the land,
but the sea, the sky, the moon, everything
in between, even what people were thinking.
I told Popeye to get to work. Popeye
flexed his muscles. He was a big, strong guy.
The audience was watching me. I waved
to their applause. Superman called me brave.

Trump, His Match

A bookstore owner in a college town
told me he's long observed his old white-haired
lady customers. Fifteen years back, scared
by George W. Bush, they weren't just down,
they wanted to die. Now facing the clown,
Trump, the ladies feel as if they've been dared
to fight: they're re-energized. How prepared
are they? Time and money to spend, they've shown
they've survived past wars—they'll endure this, too,
by phoning, writing, marching, doing what they do
to best defend their beloved country
from a grave threat within. Grandmotherly
army, they're our wisest, smartest problem-
solving citizens: don't bet against them.

Donald Trump: Dream #33

I woke. There was a growth on my temple
the size of a golf ball. It wasn't there
when I'd gone to sleep. It was so unfair,
so ugly. To hide it I wore a simple
hat and combed my hair differently. My full
head of hair was handy again. I couldn't bear
touching it, but I couldn't stop — how dare
this growth appear. This was no mere pimple —
as big as a baseball even. It felt
like it would never go away. But then
the growth started softening and shrinking.
I touched it again, hot and wet. It felt
like a thin sac tearing wide open.
Clear fluid gushed with pus. I was stinking.

Trump, Further Observed

More distinguishing characteristics:
zero empathy, a bully's bluster,
skin the color of microwaved mustard,
sense of humor like a badly thrown brick,
can't think fast or deep, doesn't read, won't fix
aberrant hair, lordly union-buster,
quick to take offense, a filthy cluster
of cellular life, can't fathom music
or joy, aimless husband, disloyal
friend, crummy parasite, chump, a royal
pain in the neck, wayward turkey, nothing
to be valued within, a thief loving
the thievery, cartoonish parade of sin,
sordid mule, ghastly pig, sullen penguin.

III

Donald Trump: The Dream After the Dreams

We were in our cars, deep in the country.
Unpaved road, lots of trees, then a clearing,
and to the left another big clearing,
and then the shooting range. I was hungry
to grab one of the guns. It cost money
to be here, but it was my understanding
we didn't have to pay. Interesting
how most of them left just as I got busy.
I loved holding the gun, aiming, shooting.
It was almost like golf — proper footing,
a target. I liked there were no women.
This place was serious. Not like swimming.
They all gave me space. Then I was alone
somehow, wearing a bull's-eye. The sun shone.

Other works by Ken Waldman

Poetry and Prose:
Nome Poems (West End Press, 2000)

To Live on This Earth (West End Press, 2002)

The Secret Visitor's Guide (Wings Press, 2006)

And Shadow Remained (Pavement Saw Press, 2006)

Conditions and Cures (Steel Toe Books, 2006)

As the World Burns (Ridgeway Press, 2006)

Are You Famous? (Catalyst Book Press, 2008)

D is for Dog Team (Nomadic Press children's poetry book, 2009)

Trump Sonnets, Volume 1 (Ridgeway Press, 2017)

Recordings:
A Week in Eek (Nomadic Press, 2000)

Burnt Down House (Nomadic Press, 2001)

Music Party (Nomadic Press, 2003)

Fiddling Poets on Parade (Nomadic Press, 2006)

All Originals, All Traditionals (Nomadic Press, 2006)

As the World Burns (Nomadic Press, 2006)

55 Tunes, 5 Poems (Nomadic Press, 2008)

Some Favorites (Nomadic Press, 2009)

D is for Dog Team (Nomadic Press, 2009)